Author Biographies

Dr. Seuss

Charlotte Guillain

www.raintreepublishers.co.uk
Visit our website to find out more information about Raintree books.

To order:
☎ Phone 0845 6044371
📄 Fax +44 (0) 1865 312263
💻 Email myorders@raintreepublishers.co.uk

Customers from outside the UK please telephone +44 1865 312262

Raintree is an imprint of Capstone Global Library Limited, a company incorporated in England and Wales having its registered office at 7 Pilgrim Street, London, EC4V 6LB – Registered company number: 6695582

Text © Capstone Global Library Limited 2012
First published in hardback in 2012
First published in paperback in 2013

Edited by Rebecca Rissman, Daniel Nunn, and Sian Smith
Designed by Joanna Hinton-Malivoire
Picture research by Tracy Cummins
Originated by Capstone Global Library Ltd
Printed in China

ISBN 978 1 406 23450 3 (hardback)
15 14 13 12 11
10 9 8 7 6 5 4 3 2 1

ISBN 978 1 406 23456 5 (paperback)
16 15 14 13 12
10 9 8 7 6 5 4 3 2 1

British Library Cataloguing in Publication Data
Guillain, Charlotte.
Dr. Seuss. – (Author biographies)
1. Seuss, Dr.–Pictorial works–Juvenile literature.
2. Authors, American–20th century–Biography–Pictorial works–Juvenile literature. 3. Illustrators–United States–Biography–Pictorial works–Juvenile literature.
I. Title II. Series
813.5'4-dc22

Acknowledgements
We would like to thank the following for permission to reproduce photographs: Alamy Images pp. 17, 22c (© Everett Collection Inc), 21, 22e (© Randy Duchaine); AP Photo pp. 9, 11 (Roswell Daily Record, Andrew Poertner), 14, 22d; Corbis pp. 4 (© James L. Amos), 13 (© KEVIN LAMARQUE/Reuters); Getty Images pp. 5, 10 (John Bryson/Time Life Pictures), 12, 16, 18 (Gene Lester); The Kobal Collection pp. 19 (MGM TV), 20, 22b (BLUE SKY/20TH CENTURY FOX); Library of Congress Prints and Photographs Division p. 6; Newscom p. 15 (HO/AFP/GETTY IMAGES); Museum of Springfield History pp. 7, 8 (Seuss Museum); Shutterstock p. 22a (© Supri Saharjoto).

Cover photograph of Theodor Seuss Geisel shaking hands with Cat in the Hat in 1988 reproduced with permission of AP Photo (Burt Steel). Back cover image of Springfield, Massachusetts in 1908 reproduced with permission of Library of Congress Prints and Photographs Division.

Contents

Some words are shown in bold, **like this**. You can find them in the glossary on page 23.

Who was Dr. Seuss?

Dr. Seuss was a writer.

He wrote and **illustrated** stories for children.

His real name was Theodor Seuss Geisel, and he wasn't really a doctor!

His most famous book is *The Cat in the Hat.*

Where did he grow up?

Dr. Seuss was born in 1904.

He grew up in a city called Springfield, in the United States.

His family had moved to the United States from Germany.

His family and friends called him Ted.

What did he do before he was a writer?

Dr. Seuss studied in the United States and England.

He started drawing cartoons when he was a student.

He got a job drawing cartoons for magazines.

Then he started drawing **advertisements**.

How did he start writing books?

Dr. Seuss's job didn't let him write books for adults.

But he was allowed to write children's books.

He wrote an ABC book but nobody would **publish** it.

But then he went on to write many popular books for children.

What books did he write?

Dr. Seuss's best-known book is *The Cat in the Hat*.

It is about a talking cat who visits some children on a rainy day.

Green Eggs and Ham is another favourite for many readers.

The book is about how it can be good to try new things.

What did he write about?

Dr. Seuss's books are very funny.

The words in his stories usually rhyme.

USA 37

THEODOR SEUSS GEISEL

2004

His books are full of strange animals and places.

He often makes readers think about how to do the right thing.

What are the pictures like in Dr. Seuss's books?

Dr. Seuss's pictures are in a cartoon style.

He drew his pictures using pen and ink.

Some of his pictures are black and white or only use a few colours.

In his later books he used more colour.

What else did he like to do?

Dr. Seuss was also an artist.

He produced many paintings and **sculptures**.

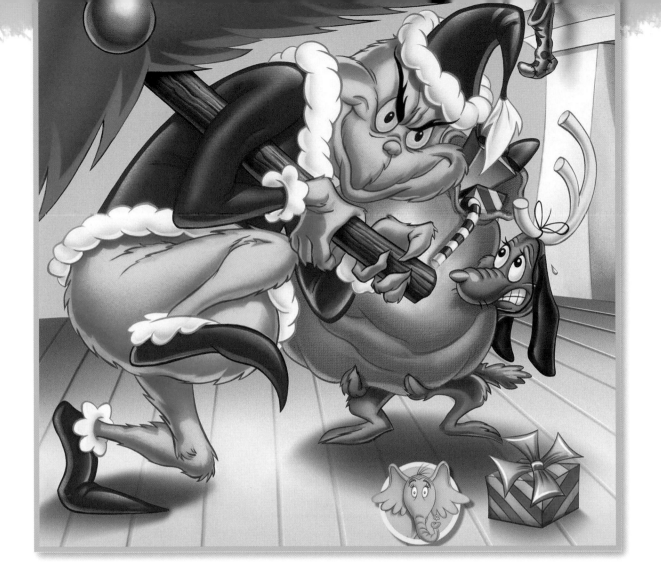

He made films when he was a
young man.

Later he helped to make films of his
stories for television.

Why is he famous today?

People still buy Dr. Seuss's books today.

His books have been made into films, cartoons, and plays.

People can visit the Dr. Seuss National Memorial Sculpture Garden in Springfield.

There are statues of Dr. Seuss and many of his **characters** there.

Timeline of Dr. Seuss's life and work

1904   Dr. Seuss was born.

1925   Dr. Seuss's first cartoon was **published**.

1937   Dr. Seuss's first book, *And to Think That I Saw It on Mulberry Street*, was published.

1957   *The Cat in the Hat* and *How the Grinch Stole Christmas!* were published.

1990   Dr. Seuss's last book, *Oh the Places You'll Go!*, was published.

1991   Dr. Seuss died.

2002   The Dr. Seuss National Memorial Sculpture Garden opened.

Glossary

 **advertisement** a picture or short film used to tell people about things they could buy

 **character** person or animal in a story

 **illustrate** draw or paint pictures to go with a story

 **publish** make into a book and have the book printed

 **sculpture** model that an artist makes, such as a statue

Find out more

Books

Some of Dr. Seuss's books: *The Cat in the Hat*, *The Cat in the Hat Comes Back*, *Green Eggs and Ham*, *How the Grinch Stole Christmas!*, *One Fish, Two Fish, Red Fish, Blue Fish*, *The Lorax*, and *Oh, the Places You'll Go!*

Websites

www.seussville.com
Visit the official Dr. Seuss website to find out more about the writer and his books, watch videos, and play games.

Index